The Stories Behind
Great Hymns

The Stories Behind Great Hymns

JAMES McCLELLAND

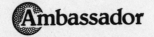

Cover photograph: Joseph Scriven's grave,
Port Hope, Ontario, Canada.
(Taken by the author)

AMBASSADOR PRODUCTIONS LTD.
241 UPPER NEWTOWNARDS ROAD,
BELFAST BT4 3JF,
NORTHERN IRELAND

Copyright (c) 1983 James McClelland
First published 1983

ISBN 0 907927 04 1

Printed in Northern Ireland by J.C. Print Ltd.

Dedication

TO MY WIFE
"Her price is far above rubies"

Acknowledgement

To all who have contributed towards the publication of this book, and to those who painstakingly typed the scripts and checked the proofs, the author gratefully acknowledges his indebtedness.

Contents

Page

Introduction

On two occasions in the New Testament the saints are exhorted to sing, "psalms, hymns and spiritual songs," and thus to make melody in their hearts to the Lord.

Psalms; refers to "songs in commemoration of mercies received." Hymns; refers to "songs in praise of God." And, spiritual songs; refers to "songs on spiritual subjects or composed by spiritual men". * There are examples of all three in this book.

Finding out the background stories to these great hymns of faith gave me a tremendous amount of personal pleasure and satisfaction. As I researched them there was aroused in me a new and consuming interest in the authors and composers. I wondered what kind of men and women they were and wanted to trace their histories wherever possible. This did become possible in one classic case: "What a friend we have in Jesus," written by Joseph Scriven.

What a thrill it was to visit Scriven's grave while on a visit to Canada in 1981. I am indebted to my brother Frank, who drove me the fifty odd miles from Toronto city, to the small hillside cemetery, overlooking Rice Lake, just outside Bewdley, Ontario.

There, on a beautifully clear day, he and I stood together and our hearts were strangely moved as we pondered the two, simple, flat, grave stones;

9

overgrown with mossy grass around the edges; partly covered with autumn leaves, and just large enough to bear their simple inscriptions. On the one - "Joseph Scriven." On the other - "Scriven's Sweetheart." What volumes of love and sadness are invisibly written there!

A large granite monument, suitably inscribed with details of Joseph Scriven's life, also graces the spot and is a fitting tribute to the life and witness of this dear saint of God. As Frank and I stood there together it was a tender, touching moment.

It is my prayer that the Lord will bless you as much in the reading of these stories as he did me in the preparation of them.

Finally, I would like to acknowledge the help of all those who supplied me with information on the various hymns; and those who helped verify or correct historic facts and dates.

James McClelland,
February, 1983.

* A Critical Lexicon and Concordance - E. W. Bullinger.

Abide With Me

In the Christian church there's a hymn for every occasion, and that's a good thing. There are hymns to encourage the saints in prayer. There are hymns of praise and testimony. There are hymns which anticipate the life to come and encourage us to look forward to heaven. And there are hymns for special seasons and occasions; Christmas, Easter, weddings and funerals.

All of us who have suffered the grief when death enters the home will understand the sense of utter helplessness into which the bereaved are plunged.

It is inevitable that the angel of death will visit every family eventually, so when he does it's important to provide the sorrowing ones with every encouragement and support that's possible.

Here's a hymn which does just that. It must have been sung at funerals more than any other hymn. There is something particularly solemn and moving about a church filled with men all singing *"Abide with me."* It seems to promote a special reverence at such times; to call down the very hush of heaven.

The man who wrote the words seemed to sense the overlapping of time and eternity; of life - and death.

Henry Francis Lyte was the pastor of a seaside congregation for more than twenty-four years. The members of his church in Lower Brixham,

11

Devonshire, on the south coast of England, were husky, hardy seafaring men; well used to wind and weather.

Well used too, to the stark trauma of tragedy at sea and the bitter cup of sudden death. The fisherfolk living in such areas of these islands are sadly familiar with the strains of *"Abide with me."*

But Pastor Lyte did not enjoy anything resembling good health. Indeed he was frail and sickly. At length it was suggested that a change of climate would be of benefit to him and accordingly he prepared to move to the sunny shores of southern Europe. The doctor gave him the grim news that he had "consumption," and advised him, "soak up all the sun you can; it's your only hope of recovery."

With more than a heavy heart the Reverend Lyte began his preparation for the journey.

Ministers become attached to their pulpits; and well nigh addicted to the ministry of the Word. Henry Francis Lyte was no exception and so, on the Sunday before he was to set sail, in September 1847, he mounted the pulpit steps once more.

The people wondered if he would have the strength to stand behind the sacred desk: and if he would have the voice to speak. However, with determination he rallied his remaining energies and addressed his beloved people: *"I stand here among you today as alive from the dead, that I may hope to impress it upon you, and induce you to prepare for that solemn hour which must come to all, by a timely acquaintance with the death of Christ."* And so he begged them once more to put their trust in the Saviour.

Later he served at the Lord's table in a communion feast with his now tearful congregation; then committed them to the Lord in prayer.

At home, that evening, anguish poured from his grief-stricken soul and in search of solace he penned the words of his now famous hymn:

"Abide with me - fast falls the eventide;
The darkness deepens; Lord, with me abide.
When other helpers fail and comforts flee,
Help of the helpless, O abide with me."

Next day the weary servant of God set sail for Nice in hope of better health. Sadly, however, it was not to be, for two months later on November 20th, he passed into the presence of the Lord with the words "joy" and "peace" upon his lips.

Henry Francis Lyte's earthly ministry had ended. He had gone to his everlasting rest and eternal reward. But, thankfully, he left behind as good a legacy as any man could hope to leave; a ministry faithfully completed and a great hymn, still sung by millions.

Amazing Grace

"March the 21st is a day to be remembered by me. I have never suffered it to pass wholly unnoticed since the year 1748. On that day the Lord sent from on high and delivered me from deep waters."

So wrote John Newton in his autobiography, aptly titled "Out of the depths." It was on that day that Newton came into a personal, saving relationship with Jesus Christ.

Ever since he was a young boy, John Newton had dreamed of following in the footsteps of his father, a sea captain. At the age of eleven his dream came true when he joined his father's ship which sailed the warm, blue waters of the Mediterranean.

Life, however, was by no means a matter of plain sailing. Growing up, the young lad soon learned the ways of wickedness - to his terrible cost. He fought with this father, clashed with his employers and finally ended up in jail. Punishment did nothing to change him, and on his release he continued his immoral living with unrestrained debauchery. Eventually, by a long sequence of tragic events, he found himself employed in one of the most despicable of all trades in those days, slavery.

But the Bible proclaims that "Christ Jesus came into the world, to save sinners." John Newton was all that - a poor, miserable, wretched sinner. And yet, it was in the Lord's great plan to save him and make something of him.

First, God brought Newton face to face with His Word. Then He followed him with His Spirit, year after year, until at last, on that memorable day in March, 1748 when a violent storm off the North-West coast of Ireland threatened to send his ship, and all aboard her, to the bottom. This caused him to fear for his very life and he called upon the Lord for mercy. It was given. John Newton was then 25 years old.

At the age of thirty-nine he became a minister of the gospel and, from that time, served the Lord and the church faithfully until his death at eighty-two.

Towards the end of his life he often told his audiences, "My memory is nearly gone but I remember two things; that I am a great sinner and that Christ is a great Saviour."

The last fifteen years of John Newton's life were spent pastoring the little church at Olney, England. During that time he and the great poet William Cowper worked together compiling a hymnbook for use by the people of God. Newton himself wrote a number of hymns, including "How sweet the name of Jesus sounds" and, most famous of all, *"Amazing grace."*

"Amazing grace" has been a firm favourite with Christians everywhere for many, many years. I'm sure it will always remain so. It is Newton's own testimony in song and tells the marvellous story of his transformation from spiritual blindness to sight - and all by grace.

On his tombstone in the little churchyard at Olney are these words: *"John Newton, clerk, once an infidel and libertine, a servant of slaves in Africa, was by the rich mercy of our Lord and Saviour, Jesus Christ, preserved, restored, pardoned and appointed to preach the faith he had long laboured to destroy."*

What else can we say than that John Newton was well qualified to preach and describe God's amazing grace.

Amazing grace! How sweet the sound,
That saved a wretch like me!
I once was lost, but now am found,
Was blind, but now I see.

'Twas grace that taught my heart to fear
And grace my fears relieved;
How precious did that grace appear
The hour I first believed.

Through many dangers, toils and snares,
I have already come;
'Tis grace hath brought me safe thus far
And grace will lead me home.

When we've been there ten thousand years,
Bright shining as the sun,
We've no less days to sing God's praise
Than when we first begun.

A Mighty Fortress

Ein feste Burg ist unser Gott,
Ein gute Wehr und Waffen.
Er hilft uns frei aus aller Not,
Die uns itzt hat betroffen.
Der alt böse Feind
Mit Ernst ers itzt meint;
Groß Macht und viel List
Sein grausam Rüstung ist,
Auf Erd ist nicht seins gleichen.

The most accurate direct translation of these words is: *"A sure stronghold our God is He: a trusty shield and weapon: our help He'll be and set us free from every ill can happen. That old malicious foe means us deadly woe: armed with might from hell and deepest craft as well: on earth is not his fellow."*

I'm sure you recognise this as the original of *"A mighty fortress is our God."*

Martin Luther, who wrote the words, once said that "The Devil hates music because he cannot stand gaiety" and "Satan can smirk but he cannot laugh; he can sneer but he cannot sing."

Because he believed in the power of song the great reformer spent a lot of time compiling a hymnbook for use in congregational singing. One writer has said that "Luther translated the Bible into German so God could speak directly to the people in His

17

word, and provided the hymnal so that the people could answer God in their songs."

Luther is credited with thirty-seven hymns, but by far the most popular is "A mighty fortress."

It was written in 1529 at a time when Luther and his followers were going through a particularly rough patch of opposition; with the Emperor Charles V seemingly determined to suppress the new movement.

During these days of struggle Luther turned often to Psalm forty-six and received much encouragement from the words of verse one: *"God is our refuge and strength, a very present help in trouble."*

Soon a song was inspired, and Luther began in fine style with the bold declaration, *"Ein feste Burg ist unser Gott"* - *"A sure stronghold our God is He."* In Frederick Hedge's translation of 1852 this became *"A mighty fortress is our God."*

Luther's original composition became immediately popular with the common people, being sung continually in the streets and chanted by the martyrs as they awaited their grim fate.

At this point mention must be made of the music, that rich melodious - yea, majestic tune which lifts the words and carries them along with all the pomp and grace of a national anthem.

Considerable dispute surrounds the origin of the music, with some attributing it to Luther himself. Others give the honour to the great J.S. Bach and it's true that Bach used the tune as the basis for one of his many chorales.

However, Bach was not born until 1685, over a hundred and fifty years after Luther's great hymn first appeared. It seems clear then, that Martin Luther deserves the credit, at least for adapting the music, possibly from an old German folk tune.

Much more important than the music however, is the message - and what a message this hymn has for the people of God. It turns their thoughts away from the afflictions of this world and the opposition of Satanic Hosts and fixes them upon the person of the Lord.

> Did we in our own strength confide,
>   Our striving would be losing;
> Were not the right Man on our side,
>   The Man of God's own choosing.
> Dost ask who that may be?
>   Christ Jesus, it is He!
> Lord Sabaoth is His name,
>   From age to age the same:
> And He must win the battle.

Blessed Assurance

The writer of this great hymn, Fanny Crosby, lived to be almost ninety-five years of age and during that time penned the staggering total of over seven thousand sacred songs and hymns.

What is even more remarkable is the fact that this great life's work was accomplished without the aid of eyesight. Due to improper medical treatment, Miss Crosby became blind when only six weeks old.

When she was twelve she entered the New York school for the blind and was so successful as a student that in later years, from 1847 until 1858, she taught at the same school.

From her prolific pen flowed such popular and all-time favourites as "Near the Cross," "Safe in the arms of Jesus," "Rescue the perishing" and *"Blessed assurance."*

The story behind the writing of *"Blessed assurance"* is simple, yet interesting.

One day Miss Crosby was in the home of her friend Mrs. Joseph F. Knapp. In the Knapp home was installed what was believed to be the largest pipe-organ ever placed in a private dwelling. However, on this particular day Mrs. Knapp called her guest over to the piano to listen to a new melody she had just composed. After playing the tune a few times she asked "What do you think the tune says?" *"Blesed assurance Jesus is mine,"* answered Fanny

Crosby, and then, drawing from her vast storehouse of scripture knowledge, she continued with *"Oh, what a foretaste of glory Divine, heir of salvation, purchase of God, born of His Spirit, washed in His blood."*

In a very short time a new sacred song was born, with words by Fanny Crosby and music by Mrs. J.F. Knapp.

Although written as far back as 1873 "Blessed assurance" still remains a firm favourite with Christians everywhere. I have personal, vivid memories of it being sung rousingly at summer beach-meetings and in the open-air, its sweet and lively strains wafting over the clear air and telling out the testimony of those who sang, *"This is my story, this is my song, Praising my Saviour all the day long."*

Perfect submission, perfect delight,
Visions of rapture burst on my sight;
Angels descending, bring from above
Echoes of mercy, whispers of love.

Perfect submission, all is at rest.
I in my Saviour am happy and blest;
Watching and waiting, looking above,
Filled with His goodness, lost in His love.

Come, Ye Thankful People, Come

One of the most beautiful seasons of the year, especially for the church, is harvest time. To see the house of God tastefully decorated with the fruits of the field and the flowers of the garden; all of them tokens of the manifold provision of God, is a sight to gladden any heart.

It's also a great opportunity to press home the truths of the scriptures to saint and sinner. Many a weary child of God has been encouraged to serve the Lord with renewed vigour; and many a wayward soul has been persuaded into the shelter of the heavenly garner, through a timely sermon on a harvest theme.

But harvest is mainly a time of praise and thanksgiving. I well remember how much sheer pleasure I experienced, as a boy, just from the singing of the harvest hymns. I don't remember a single thought from any of the harvest sermons I heard; but I do remember those lovely hymns. Hymns like "We plough the fields and scatter," "Where are the reapers," "Bringing in the sheaves," and this one *"Come, ye thankful people, come,"* bring back a flood of precious memories.

"Come, ye thankful people, come," was first published in 1844, and its original title was "After

harvest." Only the first stanza deals with the temporal harvest here on earth. The other three portray the spiritual harvest of precious souls; and the time when God shall come to "gather in" his people.

It seems clear that this hymn is based on those encouraging words in Psalm 126:6: "He that goeth forth and weepeth, bearing precious seed, shall doubtless come again with rejoicing, bringing his sheaves with him." The lines of each stanza are well worth a thoughtful perusal.

The author, the Rev. Henry Alford D.D., was born in Lordon, England, on October 7th, 1810. From all appearances he was a very godly young man. It is reported that when he was just fifteen years old he dedicated himself to the Lord in the words of this sacred vow: "I do this day, in the presence of God and my own soul, renew my covenant with God, and solemnly determine henceforth to become His and to do His work as far as in me lies." It seems that he never deviated from this for the rest of his life.

Biographers describe Henry Alford as "a pious young student, an eloquent preacher, a sound biblical critic, a man of great learning and taste, one of the most gifted men of his day, and an affectionate man, full of good humour."

His literary skills were displayed in every department of the art. He wrote a total of 50 books, the most important being his four volume "Exposition of the New Testament." It took him more than twenty years to complete.

But above all, he was a superior preacher who ever lived in the light of eternity and sought to point his listeners heavenward.

Guide Me O Thou Great Jehovah

The individual countries which together make up these beautiful British isles each has its own personal sense of national pride.

For example, Scotland, with its majestic hills and heather, its thousands of rivers, lochs and tumbling waterfalls, can be excused a certain justifiable pride in being called, "The land of the mountain and the flood."

The other countries too, have their own very good reasons for this strong national pride. I don't have time to more than mention, "Merrie England" or our own native, "Land of saints and scholars." However, I do want to talk about Wales for that's where this hymn story takes us.

Wales is, traditionally, the land of song; and the Welsh people may well be the most enthusiastic singers in all the world. In Wales, everybody loves to sing, and they sing everywhere. It always was the custom for the men to sing on their way to work in the coalmines, although that's not done so much today. But they still do fill the air with the powerful and melodious strains of their singing at rugby matches and other great outdoor events.

Soloists and choirs abound in almost every town and village. Many are well known and their music is always popular.

During the great spiritual revivals which Wales has enjoyed many times in the past two hundred years, singing and music have often played a major part. On several occasions during these revivals the preacher's sermon was interrupted by the spontaneous outburst of congregational singing and very often this was used by the Holy Spirit to move hearts to repentance and faith in the Lord Jesus.

But not only has Wales given us singers and singing in abundance, it has also raised its quota of hymn writers too.

One such was William Williams, a layman-preacher, who lived towards the end of the eighteenth century. He was a tireless servant of the Lord, and during the forty years of his ministry travelled almost 100,000 miles, on foot and on horseback, preaching and singing wherever he went.

William Williams wrote over 800 hymns, of which the best known is, *"Guide Me O Thou Great Jehovah."*

The hymn recalls some of the most trying incidents which took place during the forty-year journey of the Israelites from the bondage of Egypt to the promised land, Canaan.

What an example to us. We too, are pilgrims, on the journey from the cradle to the grave, and ultimately, to eternity. Many times our lives also seem like a wilderness - "a barren land" - as the hymn writer puts it. It is then that we must call upon the Lord to sustain us by His powerful hand.

The entire hymn is an account of God's gracious, plenteous provision for his people at every stage of life. Surely this is one of the joys of the Christian life, to know that God is with us each moment, guiding, protecting and providing.

As a result we can join with our brothers and sisters, not only in Wales, but all around the world as they sing . . . .

Guide me, O Thou great Jehovah,
  Pilgrim through this barren land;
I am weak, but Thou art mighty;
  Hold me with Thy powerful hand;
Bread of heaven,
  Feed me till I want no more.

Open now the crystal fountain,
  Whence the healing stream shall flow;
Let the fire and cloudy pillar
  Lead me all my journey through:
Strong Deliv'rer,
  Be Thou still my strength and shield.

When I tread the verge of Jordan,
  Bid my anxious fears subside;
Death of death, and hell's destruction,
  Land me safe on Canaan's side:
Songs of praises
  I will ever give to Thee!

How Great Thou Art

In Psalm 19, verse 1, King David tells us: "The heavens declare the glory of God and the firmament showeth his handiwork."

This great truth is elaborated in the words of the now-famous hymn *"How great Thou art."*

It has become one of the most popular spiritual songs of our time, and I suppose could rightly be described as a Christian classic. Its origins go back to the last century and to the majestic hills and valleys of Sweden.

Around 1885 the Rev. Carl Boberg, a well-known Lutheran minister, was 'inspired' some would say, by the natural beauty of his homeland - especially after a summer thunderstorm. He penned the words of the original poem and entitled it, "O Great God."

Mr. Boberg's words have been translated into many languages, but the version which put the hymn before the eyes of the world is the one by Stuart K. Hine.

Surely he has vividly captured the original mood of the author with the words:

"O Lord my God when I in awesome wonder,
Consider all the works Thy hands have made.
I see the stars, I hear the mighty thunder.
Thy power throughout the universe displayed.
Then sings my soul my saviour God to Thee,
How great Thou art, how great Thou art."

The music, too, is something special. The simple two-line melody of the beautiful tune is the perfect vehicle for those lovely words.

One particular verse of the hymn, more than all the others, sums up the gospel message superbly. It says:

> *"And when I think that God, His Son not sparing,*
> *   Sent Him to die, I scarce can take it in.*
> *That on the Cross, my burden gladly bearing,*
> *   He bled and died to take away my sin.*
> *Then sings my soul my saviour God to Thee,*
> *   How great Thou art, how great Thou art."*

Surely here's a hymn of praise that everyone can sing.

I Heard The Voice Of Jesus Say

This hymn has been referred to as one of the most ingenious in the English language. Each stanza divides equally between invitation and response. For example, the first stanza begins with the picture of a weary soul in search of rest from the burden of sin; but concludes with the heart's glad response to the Saviour's invitation to "Come unto me." Similar comparisons and contrasts are easily seen in the other two stanzas.

The author of this hymn, Dr. Horatius Bonar, was born in Edinburgh, Scotland, on December 19th, 1808. He was ordained to the ministry of the Church of Scotland, then established, in 1837, but left at the Disruption in 1843 to become one of the founders of the Free Church. In that same year he married Miss Jane Lundie and moved to a pastorate in Kelso, on the river Tweed, in the Scottish borders.

Their 40 years together were not without trouble and sorrow, yet they could testify that all these things brought glory to God and gave them a wider ministry. When five of their children died early in life, Horatious wrote, "Spare not the stroke; do with us as Thou wilt; let there be naught unfinished, broken, marred. Complete Thy purpose, that we may become Thy perfect image." Surely, the sign of true godliness.

It is reported that Dr. Bonar spent many hours each day in his study, praying aloud. A maid, who was converted in his home through these prayers, commented, "If *he* needs to pray so much, what will happen to me if *I* don't pray."

Once, when speaking to a young man about the matter of his salvation, he discovered that this individual had great difficulty in believing that the Lord could, and would save him from his sin. Dr. Bonar asked, "Which is of greater weight - your sin, or the blood of Jesus; shed for sinners?" Joyfully the young man answered, "I am sure the blood of Jesus weighs more heavily than even my sin." Thus, by the wisdom and skill of the man of God he was brought to saving faith in Christ. Dr. Bonar firmly believed that the antidote to crimson sin is the cleansing blood of Jesus.

He was a prolific writer, editing two magazines, publishing many articles and producing hundreds of tracts. One of these, entitled, "Believe and live," and said to be a favourite of Queen Victoria, sold a million copies. He also wrote 600 hymns and translated at least 60 Psalms.

He was a man with a powerful and consecrated intellect, a deep knowledge of the Scriptures, and a physical stature both tall and strong. But these somewhat overpowering characteristics were offset by a gentle, sympathetic nature and a childlike faith.

Perhaps it was this childlikeness which gave him such a love for children. Certainly it was his love and concern for the young that led him to the writing of hymns. When he observed their rather indifferent spirit towards the traditional singing of the Psalms; but a much livelier attitude when singing their weekday songs, he decided to write sacred words for their joyful tunes. The experiment met with instant success, and brought excellent results. One woman, who had attended his Wednesday Bible class, later testified, "We still cherish the hymn he wrote specially for us." It ran . . .

"Shall this life of mine be wasted?
Shall this vineyard lie untilled?
Then, no longer idly dreaming,
Shall I fling my years away;
But, each precious hour redeeming,
Wait for the eternal day."

In 1866 Horatious Bonar moved to Edinburgh, the city of his birth, where he continued his labours for the Master until his death on July 31st, 1889.

I heard the voice of Jesus say,
"Come unto Me and rest;
Lay down, thou weary one, lay down
Thy head upon My breast."

I came to Jesus as I was—
Weary, and worn, and sad;
I found in Him a resting place,
And He has made me glad.

I Need Thee Every Hour

Several of the hymn stories in this book relate the trying experiences of the children of God, and how those afflictions have been the material from which great hymns were written.

But here's one which came into being under completely different circumstances and makes a refreshing change.

Annie Sherwood Hawks was born in Hoosick, New York, on 28th May, 1835. Even from an early age she was writing poetry, and at 14 had some published in a newspaper. When she married, at 24, she moved to live in the Brooklyn area of New York. There, she and her husband joined the church whose pastor was the noted hymn writer and composer, Dr. Robert S. Lowry.

Dr. Lowry recognised Mrs. Hawks talent for writing and encouraged her to use it. In fact, he even offered her a challenge. "If you'll write the words, I'll write the music," he said, and he was as good as his word.

"I need thee every hour" was written in April 1872 and is thought to have been based on John 15:4 & 5. It was first performed in November 1872 at the National Baptist Sunday School Convention at Cincinatti. However, very soon it was taken up by the famous evangelistic team, Moody and Sankey, who, I suppose, did most to make it popular. It was

also translated into many languages and even featured at the Chicago World's Fair.

A short time before her death which took place on January 3rd, 1918, Mrs. Hawks gave the background story to the writing of her hymn. I quote her own words. "I remember well the circumstances under which I wrote the hymn. It was a bright June day, and I became so filled with the sense of the nearness of my Master that I began to wonder how one could live without Him in either joy or pain. Suddenly the words, *'I need Thee every hour,'* flashed into my mind; and very quickly the thought had full possession of me. Seating myself by the open windows, I caught up my pencil and committed the words to paper - almost as they are today. A few months later Dr. Robert Lowry composed the tune 'Need' for my hymn and also added the refrain."

"For myself, the hymn, at its writing, was prophetic rather than expressive of my own experiences; for it was wafted out to the world on the wings of love and joy, instead of under the stress of great personal sorrow, with which it has so often been associated. At first I did not understand why the hymn so greatly touched the throbbing heart of humanity. Years later, however, under the shadow of a great loss, I came to understand something of the comforting power of the words I had been permitted to give out to others in my hours of sweet serenity and peace."

It must have given her great satisfaction to write a hymn that has been such a blessing to so many people.

I Think When I Read That Sweet Story

Like quite a number of other hymns we have considered, this one began life on the back of an envelope. That was away back in 1841; and it happened like this.

The author, Jemima Thompson, had been spending some time at an infant school gaining knowledge of the system. As the teachers and children marched around the schoolroom, Miss Thompson was intrigued by the melody of the tune they kept time to. It turned out to be a Greek air called "Salamis," and immediately a search began to find appropriate words for this beautiful music. However, although several hymnals were consulted no suitable words were found.

Sometime later, while riding alone on a stage coach, Jemima began to hum the haunting melody. Suddenly, the words we are now so familiar with, began to form in her heart and mind, and, taking an envelope from her bag she quickly jotted them down. Very soon she taught the new words to her school children and the following Sunday they sang them in Miss Thompson's father's church.

He was delighted at the sound and when he asked who had written the lovely words received the answer from the happy children, "Jemima did."

Next day the Rev. Thompson sent the words to 'The Sunday School Teachers Magazine,' and they were printed immediately.

Jemima Thompson was born near London, England on August 19th 1813. She came to Christ as Saviour at the tender age of ten and by the time she was thirteen was already writing for a periodical called, 'The Juvenile Magazine.' Later, she edited the first ever missionary magazine for children, 'The Missionary Repositary,' which received contributions from such famous missionary names as, David Livingstone, James Moffat, and James Montgomery.

Jemima herself, had plans to go to India as a missionary to women, but ill health prevented her from ever setting sail.

In 1843 she married the Reverend Samuel Luke, a congregational minister, and devoted herself to her duties as 'lady of the manse,' as well as to further writing.

However, it is for this one hymn that she is best known. It is probably true to say that by means of it she has reached multitudes for the Lord and has inspired many to answer God's call to service on the mission field.

Jemima Thompson Luke finally said farewell to this world in 1906, at the age of 93. Her earthly ministry was ended but her memory will live on forever in the words of her beautiful hymn.

I think when I read that sweet story of old,
*   When Jesus was here among men,*
How He call'd little children as lambs to His fold,
*   I should like to have been with Him then.*

It Is Well With My Soul

The prophet Isaiah records that, God keeps in perfect peace all who trust in Him. (Isa. 26:3). Nowhere is this truth more aptly illustrated than in the story which accompanies the writing of the hymn *"It is well with my soul."*

Horatio G. Spafford lived in Chicago with his wife and four daughters. He was a lawyer by profession; and also a sincere Christian.

In 1873, he said farewell to his wife and family as they set sail from Chicago to visit relatives in Europe. Some days later, their ship, bound for Le Havre in France, collided in mid-Atlantic with another steamship and sank almost immediately.

Before it did so, however, Mrs. Spafford was able to have prayer with her children and commit them to the mercy of the Lord. She was never to see them, on this earth, again.

Fortunately, a lifeboat spotted Mrs. Spafford and she was rescued. When she arrived in Britain, with the rest of the survivors, she sent her husband this terse, but telling, message: *"Saved - Alone."*

The words struck Horatio Spafford with full force and, understandably, plunged him into deep sorrow. He left immediately for England, to comfort his grief-stricken wife.

It is interesting to note that evangelist D. L. Moody and singer Ira D. Sankey, who were good friends of the Spaffords and were conducting a campaign in Edinburgh at the time; came to London to give whatever comfort they could. They found their friends in surprisingly good spirit; strong in faith and able to say through their tears *"It is well; the will of God be done."*

Three years after that tragedy at sea, Mr. Spafford wrote the hymn *"It is well with my soul,"* in memory of his four precious daughters. Happily, each of them had personally received Christ as Saviour before they embarked on that fateful voyage.

It would be very difficult for any of us to predict how we would react under circumstances similar to those experienced by the Spaffords. But we know that the God Who sustained them will also be with us.

Unclouded skies and gentle winds do not test our vessel of faith; it takes the storm and the tempest to prove the strength of our trust in Him. No matter what circumstances overtake us may we be able to say with Horatio Spafford:

> *"When peace, like a river, attendeth my way,*
> *When sorrows like sea billows roll;*
> *Whatever my lot, Thou hast taught me to say,*
> *It is well, it is well with my soul."*

Jesus Lover Of My Soul

No study of the great hymns of the Christian faith would be complete without a look at the work of the one man who did more for English hymns than any other - Charles Wesley.

Even though his father was a clergyman, Charles Wesley grew up without ever coming to a knowledge of sins forgiven or the assurance of salvation. Thankfully, however, like his famous brother John, he finally found spiritual peace through the help of the Moravians, especially that of Peter Böhler who explained to him the nature of justification by faith alone. Thus it was that on Whit Sunday, May 21st 1738, Charles Wesley found peace with God through our Lord Jesus Christ.

From that time he was as much on fire to preach the gospel as his brother; and equally bold and tireless in doing so. Above all, he translated the gospel message into song, furnishing both a powerful means of evangelism and a rich reservoir of devotion.

On the first anniversary of his conversion he wrote those majestic lines:-

> *"Oh for a thousand tongues, to sing*
> *My great Redeemer's praise,*
> *The glories of my God and King*
> *The triumphs of His grace!"*

These lines have been used to open successive editions of the Methodist hymn book ever since.

Hymn writing came easy to Charles Wesley, anytime, anywhere, so that from his busy pen there flowed some nine thousand sacred songs. Christendom still sings many of them. Compositions like *"Love divine all loves excelling,"* *"Christ the Lord is risen today, Hallelujah,"* and *"Hark the herald angels sing"* are still firm favourites with believers all around the globe.

Today we are considering one of the most popular of all - and one of the most beautiful - *"Jesus lover of my soul,"* which was written just two years after he came to know the Lord as his saviour. Strange as it may seem, this hymn was not afforded a place in any Methodist hymnal until nine years after the author's death because his brother John thought it much too sentimental to be used as a spiritual song.

No one is really sure what experience prompted the writing of the lovely words, but it is certain that something did. Some say that a little bird flew into Wesley's room for protection and then sought refuge inside the folds of his coat, thus giving him the idea of believers flying to the Lord's bosom for *their* protection.

But whatever did, or did not happen, Charles Wesley's prayer-poem has found a responsive chord in the ears, and hearts, of tens of thousands.

Jesus Loves Me

One of the most delightful things for any minister is to have a church with plenty of children and young people. What life and laughter and fun they bring about the place! They seem to be always happy; they're so often full of excitement; and— *they're nearly always good!*

I like their cute little faces, their wide excited eyes and their simple, trusting ways. I like their singing too. There is something special about the lisping, lilting voices of children that touches the heart.

Of course, the hymn which is most closely associated with children is *"Jesus loves me."*

It was written in 1859 by Susan and Anna Warner who were the daughters of a New York lawyer. The two young women were talented writers and in 1859 published a novel entitled "Say and Seal." It became a best seller.

However, even the very best of novels remain popular for only a limited time, and "Say and Seal" eventually went the way of all the rest. But, as long as *"Jesus loves me"* is still sung by children it will never be entirely forgotten. The poem, which is now an all time favourite hymn, first appeared within the pages of the Warner girls' novel.

In "Say and Seal", two of the characters, Faith Derrick and John Endecott Linden are greatly concerned for a very sick little fellow named,

Johnny Fax. Johnny's condition becomes critical and he asks Mr. Linden, who was also the Sunday School teacher, to take him up in his strong arms and comfort him. Mr. Linden readily does so, and picking up the feverish little boy, walks slowly back and forth across the room trying to console him.

Suddenly, Johnny pleads, "Sing".

As Faith listens, she hears John Linden sing a beautiful song which neither she nor Johnny have ever heard before . . .

> *"Jesus loves me, this I know,*
> *For the Bible tells me so*
> *Little ones to Him belong*
> *They are weak, but He is strong."*

With this he sought to comfort the final moments of the dying lad. Indeed, a few hours later, little Johnny Fax went to be with the one who loved him so much.

The lines of the poem came to the attention of the famous composer, William Bradbury, and in 1861 he set them to music and added the chorus . . .

> *"Yes Jesus loves me, yes Jesus loves me;*
> *Yes Jesus loves me; the Bible tells me so."*

Jesus Thy Blood And Righteousness

The family of Count Nicholas Ludvig Von Zinzendorf was one of the wealthiest in Saxony. So when the young nobleman wound up his law studies in the university of Wittenberg he set out to see the world in luxury. But he got only as far as an art gallery in Dusseldorf. There, pondering a painting of Christ with His bowed head and the inscription *"This have I done for thee, what hast thou done for Me"* the count was smitten with conviction. He went back to his estate at Berthelsdorf with a heavy heart, and miserable. But God was dealing with him. At twenty-two, on his wedding day, he and his bride put aside their rank of nobility to follow in the footsteps of the lowly man of Galilee.

Shortly after this a religious outcast named Christian David wandered into Berthelsdorf. Christian David belonged to the society known as "The Moravian Brethren." The Moravians had been founded some three hundred years earlier by John Huss, known in history books as "The Old Goose of Bohemia."

Count Zinzendorf took David in and rounded up all the other brethren he could find so that within ten years, six hundred Moravians were living on his estate. The Count organised the Moravians into missionary groups and sent them off to the far corners of the earth.

To Greenland, Holland, India, America and the Indies these pioneers of missionary endeavour went forth with holy zeal. Long before William Carey put down his cobblers last to take up his Bible and long before John and Charles Wesley preached a sermon or wrote a hymn, the Moravians had one hundred and sixty-five missions scattered around the world. They faced disease, poverty, loneliness and persecution but nothing stopped them from carrying on the work of the crucified Christ, whose picture their leader had seen in a gallery at Dusseldorf.

On December 21st 1741, Zinzendorf founded a mission and preached to the Indians in Pennsylvania. As it was only four days to Christmas he named the colony, Bethlehem. It's a great steel centre today and the Moravian capital of the United States.

The Count *saw* the world - but not in luxury. When he died, back in his native Saxony, aged sixty, there wasn't enough money to pay for his grave.

Zinzendorf wrote 2,000 hymns during his long life of service for Christ. In 1739, while on board a ship on the way to establish a mission in the West Indies, he wrote this beautiful hymn:

> *Jesus Thy blood and righteousness*
> *My beauty are, my glorious dress*
> *'Midst flaming worlds, in these arrayed*
> *With joy shall I lift up my head.*

When I think of all that Count Zinzendorf gave up and all he endured for the sake of Christ's kingdom I am bound to be persuaded that he meant everything he wrote.

Just As I Am

It must be true to say that no sacred song or hymn has been more used to bring sinners to the feet of Jesus, than this one.

Sung by grand choirs in vast crusades as hundreds have come; or by congregations large and small as one's and two's have come; this hymn has moved the hearts of multitudes.

"Just as I am," rings with a clear, positive note. It invites the sinner to come just as he is; with all his sin; in all his unworthiness; despite his fears; though poor, wretched and blind; to come to the Saviour.

That's an invitation which is absolutely scriptural. We don't need to wait until our lives have been straightened out before we come to Christ. There's nothing we can do which will ever make us more acceptable in God's sight. The Bible clearly teaches that God loves the sinner, just the way he is, and wants him to come like that.

Only Jesus Christ can deliver us from the guilt and penalty of sin. Only He can solve all the problems of life. Only He can give us peace and joy and hope for the future.

It was out of her own feelings of frustration and hopelessness that the author, Charlotte Elliott, wrote the words of this fine hymn.

One day in 1833, when Miss Elliott was in her forty-fourth year, she was feeling unusually depressed and alone. The other members of her family had gone off to a church function while she, an invalid and bedridden, remained at home. Before her illness she had lived a happy, carefree life; enjoying its many pleasures and gaining a measure of popularity as a portrait artist.

Now all of this past, and stricken with the sickness which was to plague her for the rest of her life, she felt utterly useless and cut off. In addition, although she had been a Christian for many years, she began to have doubts about her relationship with the Lord. How could she be sure that all was well with her soul?

In her distress she began to list scriptural reasons for believing that she was, indeed, a child of God. She recognised the power of the Saviour's precious blood. She remembered His promise to receive all who come to Him by faith; and His ability to pardon, cleanse and save.

As she meditated on these great truths her heart was warmed and very soon Charlotte Elliott, who was also fond of writing poetry, was putting down her thoughts in verse:

> *"Just as I am, without one plea*
> *But that Thy blood was shed for me,*
> *And that Thou bidd'st me come to Thee,*
> *O Lamb of God, I come, I come."*

William H. Bradbury, mentioned elsewhere in this book as the composer of the music for, *"Sweet hour of prayer,"* heard of Miss Elliott's poem. His heart was also warmed by the grand old gospel truths so well expressed in rhyme. He liked the way the poet had emphasised the importance of claiming

Christ's merits as the means of finding peace with God. It wasn't long, then, until he had composed a melody and set the words to it.

Charlotte Elliott never did enjoy good health for the rest of her life. She remained bedridden until the Lord, at last, called her home when she was eighty-two. But before her death she received more than a thousand letters of thanks and compliment from people who were grateful that she had written, *"Just as I am."*

As Nathanael Olson points out; here's an example of how the Lord can take someone who feels completely "useless" and make them "useful for Him!"

Just as I am — Thy love unknown
Has broken ev'ry barrier down;
Now to be Thine, yea, Thine alone,
O Lamb of God, I come, I come.

Leaning On The Everlasting Arms

There was a time in America when only those who could afford private lessons were able to sing by music. There were few songbooks, and church-goers depended on songleaders to set the tune of the hymn and call out the words, line by line, while the congregations sang after them. It's still done in the highlands of Scotland to this day at funerals and certain other occasions.

But back to our American story. Through the persistent representations of a musician called Lowell Mason music became an official subject in the schools. Songbooks were published and trained music-masters were sent into rural America to teach the people how to sing. Professor A.J. Showalter was one such music-master.

One day in 1887, after music class had been dismissed he collected his books, locked up the church house where they met and made his way across town to the boarding house where he had put up for his brief stay in Hartselle, Alabama.

When he arrived, two letters from former students in South Carolina were waiting for him.

Showalter read the first letter. It brought the sad news that this student had just suddenly lost his wife. The professor left the letter aside and decided to answer it later.

Opening the second one he found that it brought news identical to that of the first. What a tragic coincidence. Two former students had each been plunged into tragedy, through the same circumstances, and on the same day.

In an effort to console his two young friends Showalter wrote: *"The eternal God is thy refuge and underneath are the everlasting arms."* He paused, and put down his pen.

In that single line of Scripture lay the theme of a great hymn. His pupils could read music, and they could sing - for he had taught them. Then why not write them a *"song"* of comfort instead of a letter? Quickly he wrote the chorus:

"Leaning, leaning, safe and secure from all alarms,
Leaning, leaning, leaning on the everlasting arms."

Professor Showalter sent the chorus off to the Rev. Elisha Hoffman in Pennsylvania, and Hoffman - himself the author of over 2,000 hymns - very soon produced three beautiful verses.

When Showalter received Hoffman's finished work he wrote the music for it, and another great hymn was born.

We don't have any record of what effect the song message had on those for whom it was written, but we do know it has been a great blessing to thousands ever since.

What have I to dread, what have I to fear,
Leaning on the everlasting arms;
I have blessed peace with my Lord so near,
Leaning on the everlasting arms.

Let The Lower Lights Be Burning

I love the sea! I love boats! There's nothing gives me more pleasure than to take my own little boat down to the water and spend a few hours just pottering about.

One of my favourite sailing spots is the beautiful area of Carlingford Lough in County Down, where the air is bracing and the scenery majestic. But the tides there are strong; and the currents can be very treacherous. You really do need to know what you are doing and, perhaps more important, where you are going.

I was very fortunate then, that a good friend of mine, who is also a keen sailor, went with me when I first ventured onto Carlingford. He came to show me the way around and to point out "the marks", as they call them. The few hours he spent with me that day, sailing from Greencastle, over to Carlingford harbour, down by the Black House, and out as far as the lighthouse at Cranfield, and pointed out the navigation marks on the way, were greatly appreciated. I can now sail that stretch of water with complete confidence, because I know the danger spots; and how to stay clear of them.

How important it is to be able to find your way, especially in treacherous circumstances. That's what

D. L. Moody must have had in mind when he told the following story.

On a dark and stormy night in the last century, when the waves rolled like mountains and not a single star lit the darkness of the sky, a large passenger ship cautiously edged its way towards the harbour at Cleveland, Ohio. On board, the pilot knew that, on such a night, he could only find the safety of the harbour by keeping the two lower shore lights in line with the main beacon.

"Are you sure this is Cleveland?" asked the captain, who could see only one light, that from the lighthouse.

"Yes, I'm quite sure," replied the pilot, peering into the inky darkness.

"But, where are the lower lights?" asked the captain.

"They must have gone out, sir," came the reply.

"Can you still make the harbour then?" enquired the now anxious captain.

"We must, or perish, sir," said the pilot solemnly, as he swung the wheel again.

With a strong hand and a brave heart the old pilot steered the heaving vessel onward. But alas! In the darkness he missed the vital channel, the boat crashed on the rocks, and many lives were lost.

When Mr. Moody first told the story of the shipwreck at Cleveland, he concluded with these words, *"Brethren, the Master will take care of the great lighthouse; let us keep the lower lights burning."*

That story fired the imagination of one of Dr. Moody's associates, Philip Bliss. He was already a song writer and composer of some repute; and when he took the moral of this story and told it in song, it

50

became popular immediately. Soon, *"Let the lower lights be burning,"* was being sung in Moody campaigns everywhere. Later it was to become a firm favourite with that other famous American evangelist, Billy Sunday.

We all meet with people every day, and for those people we may provide the only opportunity they will ever have to hear the gospel. Unless we tell them, they may never hear!

I'm sure that's what Philip Bliss had in mind when he penned the last verse of his hymn. In exhorting us to show others the way of salvation it speaks of lamps of a different, but equally important kind, and reminds me of something from my childhood days.

I grew up on my father's small farm and one of things I remember clearly is, the "hurricane" lamp. Those were the days before electricity came to our part of the country, so if you had any work to do outside at night, a lamp was essential. "Hurricanes," were the most popular.

These had a wide metal base and a strong carrying handle; they used paraffin oil, and had a wick which was totally enclosed in a storm-proof, glass globe. Hence, the name "Hurricane".

From time to time, when the light would grow dim, my father would dismantle the lamps to clean them.

The globe would be washed, then polished with newspaper until it sparkled. The wick would be trimmed, removing all the charred edges, and neatly shaped to give a nice oval flame. Then the lamp would be refilled with fresh oil; and lighted. It was

51

almost a pleasure to go out on a dark, winter night with a "hurricane" which had received this treatment.

I feel that's the type of lamp Philip Bliss was referring to when he wrote:

> *"Trim your feeble lamp, my brother;*
> *Some poor sailor tempest-tossed,*
> *Trying now to make the harbour,*
> *In the darkness may be lost."*

Jesus expressed the same thought in an almost identical way when He said, *"Let your light so shine before men, that they may see your good works, and glorify your Father which is in heaven."*

Nearer, My God, To Thee

I used to work as a messenger boy for a Belfast firm of industrial suppliers. One of our biggest customers was the mighty Queen's Island shipyard; so almost every week found me down there, in one department or another, delivering everything from goggles to grommets.

I used to love to walk through the busy engine works and see the building and testing of those monstrous mechanical wonders that would one day find a place in the depths of some great ocean-going vessel; and drive it through the waves with speed and power.

Sometimes, on a good day, I stood and watched the actual building of a ship. It was an amazing sight for a country lad to see gigantic pieces of sheet metal being swung through the air and then gently set into place by the skill of the crane-man. To this day I can hear the deafening and monotonous rat-tat-tat of the riveting machines; and see the dazzling blue flashing of the electric arc welders as, sheet by sheet, a great ship was put together.

The "Island" is renowned for its ships; many with famous and historic names. I remember the building of the "Canberra", and recollect how proud she looked as she lay at her moorings while being fitted out. I remember, too, the building of the first oil rig;

an absolutely monstrous structure and, at that time, an eighth wonder of the world.

But I suppose the most famous, and sadly, the most tragic of all the vessels built at Belfast was the "Titanic", which sank, on her maiden voyage, on that fateful night in April 1912.

Many stories are told about that night of terror but surely one of the most poignant is the account of how the band, which all evening had played music to dance to, finally, just as the ship was about to slide beneath the icy waters, broke into the strains of a famous hymn.

The one they chose was *"Nearer, my God, to Thee."*

The inspiration for this timeless favourite came to the author through the reading of the scriptures, in particular, the story of Jacob at Bethel. (Gen. 28:10-22).

As Sarah Flower Adams read the moving story, a prayer was born in her heart and she longed to be drawn nearer to her Lord. She composed the lines of her hymn in November 1840.

It was said to be the favourite hymn of President William McKinley. As he lay dying, after being shot in Buffalo, New York, he was heard to whisper *"Nearer, my God, to Thee . . . nearer, my God, to Thee."*

Sarah Flower inherited her love for and ability with words from her father who was a newspaper editor. She was born in England in 1805 and teamed with her sister, Eliza, in writing and publishing sacred songs. *"Nearer, my God, to Thee,"* first appeared in 1841 in their book "Hymns and Anthems."

It's interesting to note that the most popular tune for *"Nearer, my God, to Thee,"* Lowell Mason's "Bethany" is an arrangement of a beautiful old Irish ballad "Oft in the stilly night."

Sarah Flower Adams was taken ill with the then dreaded consumption and passed away at the age of forty-three.

Her hymn, however, has lived on for more than a hundred and forty years.

> *Nearer, my God, to Thee,*
> *Nearer to Thee;*
> *E'en though it be a cross*
> *That raiseth me;*
> *Still all my song shall be,*
> *Nearer, my God, to Thee,*
> *Nearer to Thee.*

O Come, All Ye Faithful

John Francis Wade was an itinerant scribe. In those days long ago, when printing was still in its infancy and a rather slow way of reproducing copies of a work, he roamed from town to town offering his services to those who could pay for them.

Wade was a craftsman of the highest order, working in several languages and able also to copy music manuscripts. Consequently, his copywriting was much in demand by choir leaders, institutions of learning, churches and wealthy families.

He worked mostly in his native England but also ventured as far afield as France and some of the Western European countries to ply his trade there.

Apparently however, Scribe Wade didn't spend all his time copying the works of others. In 1750, as part of a manuscript he prepared for a college in Lisbon, Portugal, he included an original composition from his own pen.

It was written in the Latin language and began . . .

"Adeste, fideles,
Laeit triumphantes;
Venite, venite in Bethlehem . . ."

In English, it's the very popular , . .

"O come, all ye faithful, joyful and triumphant,
O come ye, O come ye to Bethlehem . . ."

Wade also composed a fine tune for the words he had written, and when the two were blended they produced an extraordinary musical composition. It's sung with great enthusiasm in churches all over the world at Christmas.

In 1785 the carol was heard by the then Duke of Leeds. He introduced it to a group of concert singers of which he was the conductor and it increased in popularity from that time.

Eventually it circled the globe, being translated into every civilized language on the way. In the past century for example, it has appeared in over one hundred different English translations.

However, it was not until 1852, and the translation by Canon Frederick Oakley of Shrewsbury, that it became known by its present popular title *"O come, all ye faithful."*

It should be pointed out that some historians assert that John Francis Wade was not, in fact, the author of this carol. They say he borrowed both the words and the music from others whose names we will never know.

But whether or not Wade was guilty of plagarism, it is undeniable that this moving carol would never have come into the possession of the Christian church had he not inserted it into that ancient manuscript.

> *Amen! Lord, we bless Thee,*
> *Born for our salvation,*
> *O Jesus! forever be Thy name adored;*
> *Word of the Father,*
> *Now in flesh appearing.*
>
> *O come, let us adore Him,*
> *Christ the Lord!*

O Little Town Of Bethlehem

The Reverend Phillips Brooks spent Christmas 1865 in Bethlehem, the town where the baby Jesus was born. The sights and sounds of the ancient city flooded into his keen mind leaving indelible impressions. Three years later these impressions would be enshrined in a hymn he would write especially for the children of his Sunday School.

Phillips Brooks was a big man, physically, mentally and spiritually. He is said to have been one of the biggest preachers of his day, standing six foot six in height with a weight to match. Clint Bonner tells us that *"he sang 200 hymns from memory and blasted out sermons at a rate of 250 words per minute."*

The story of the hymn he wrote goes back to a December day in 1868 when the massive preacher paced the study of the Episcopal Church in Philadelphia, where he was the minister.

It was just a few days before Christmas; and Brooks was working on a sermon especially for the season. Out in the church the organist and Sunday School superintendant, Lewis Redner, practiced carols and special music for the forthcoming Christmas services.

As the preacher walked up and down his thoughts took him back to Bethlehem and the shepherds watching over their sheep just as they did when Jesus was born.

58

He laid aside his sermon preparation and took up his pen. The words: *"O little town of Bethlehem, how still we see thee lie"* flowed quickly and in a short time he had completed the four verses.

He asked Redner to write a tune. The organist made no claim to be a composer but agreed to have a go. The days passed, until it was almost Christmas, but Redner still didn't have any ideas for the music. Then something quite amazing happened!

On the night before Christmas, just about midnight, he was awakened, *"as though by an angel strain."* *"The music seemed to come down from heaven"* Redner later recorded, and he quickly jotted down the melody. Just as quickly as he was awakened, he went back to sleep; and finished the harmonies for the tune in the morning. Later that same day he taught it to the children of the Sunday School.

It must have been a great thrill for those children to sing *"O little town of Bethlehem,"* the first time it was ever heard on that Christmas day in 1868.

Phillips Brooks continued his ministry for another 25 years, eventually becoming Bishop of Massachusetts. He remained a bachelor; but never lost his love for, and way with, children. It seems they loved him too, for, when he died, in Boston in 1893, one little 5-year-old girl said, with tears in her eyes, *"How happy the angels will be."*

The angel's gain was the children's loss. But at least Bishop Brooks left something really precious to be remembered by.

O Love That Wilt Not Let Me Go

We often wonder why it is that God allows His saints to suffer so much hardship. Yet, it's true that He does. The latter part of Hebrews chapter eleven is proof positive, if such proof is needed, that this is so.

However, God has a purpose in everything. He doesn't do things by whim or by chance. Everything is reasoned and planned, and for the very best of motives. When He does ask His child to endure hardship, it is never out of malice or spite, but that the believer may learn to trust Him more.

Yet, it's wonderful how so many of these trials become triumphs; and how seemingly impossible situations turn into milestones of blessing.

Surely, one such is the experience which led George Matheson to write those lovely words *"O love that wilt not let me go."*

George Matheson was born in Glasgow, Scotland, on 27th March 1842. Before he was very old it was discovered that he suffered from a disease which would eventually cause him to become completely blind. Despite this, he pressed on with his studies, and, in due course entered university; finishing there, with honours, when he was 19.

It was while at university that he suffered the stunning blow which later prompted the writing of his beautiful hymn.

He had met and fallen in love with a young woman, also a student at university, and it appears they had planned to be married. But then George had to tell her the awful news that one day he would be blind. Would she still marry him?

To his astonishment and grief her blunt answer came, striking to his heart with the force of a dagger: *"I do not want to be the wife of a blind man."* And with that they parted.

Years later the memory of that rebuff came flooding back on the eve of his sister's wedding; and in less than five minutes he penned these immortal words. Matheson recorded that they were *"The fruit of suffering, written when I was alone and suffering a mental anguish over something that no one else knew."*

This story will surely strike a sympathetic chord in the heart of every reader. Who among us would care to suffer the deep personal hurt which was George Matheson's; yet who among us has not been blessed by the words which were born out of that desperate experience?

That George Matheson triumphed over his great disappointment is evident. After leaving university he spent another four years in the study of theology, preparing himself for the ministry.

His first pastorate was at Innellan on the Clyde, where he stayed for 18 years. It was while there that he received a summons to preach before Her Majesty, Queen Victoria. The Queen was so impressed both by his preaching and prayers that she presented him with a small sculpture of herself.

She had the thoughtfulness not to present a blind man with a photograph.

His ministry continued, long, faithful and fruitful, until August 28th 1906, when, on a much needed holiday, he was called home to be with his Saviour. His body was laid to rest in the family vault at Glasgow.

Some would say that much of the success of *"O love that wilt not let me go,"* results from the tune "Saint Margaret." It was composed by Dr. Albert L. Peace; who was organist at Glasgow Cathedral and it came to him while sitting on the sandy shores of the Arran Island.

O Love, that wilt not let me go,
  I rest my weary soul in Thee;
I give Thee back the life I owe,
  That in Thine ocean depths, it flow
May richer, fuller be.

O Perfect Love

Thousands of people at thousands of weddings must have sung this popular and moving hymn, without knowing the simple story behind its composition.

"O Perfect Love," was written in 1883, by Dorothy Frances Bloomfield Gurney; and all in the space of about fifteen minutes. According to Mrs. Gurney, relating the story years later, it happened like this:

"It was Sunday evening and we were enjoying a time of hymn singing. A song that was particularly enjoyed by us all was 'O Strength and Stay.' As we finished someone remarked, 'What a pity the words of this beautiful song are not suitable for a wedding!' My sister turned to me and challenged, 'What's the use of a sister who composes poetry if she cannot write new words to a favourite tune? I would like to use this tune at my wedding.' I picked up a hymnbook and said, 'If no one will disturb me, I'll go into the library and see what I can do.' Within fifteen minutes I was back with the group and reading the words I had jotted down. The writing of them was no effort after the initial idea came to me. I feel God helped me write this song."

Some two or three years after its original composition, "O Perfect Love," found its way into the well known hymnal, "Hymns Ancient and

Modern." Possibly, because of this, it soon became popular, especially in London, where it was used at many fashionable weddings, including those of royalty.

In 1889, Sir Joseph Barnaby composed a new tune with the appropriate name, "Sandringham," and the hymn was sung to this tune when Princess Louise of Wales, daughter of King George V, was married to the Duke of Fife.

Since then the hymn has been translated into many languages and has attained worldwide fame. Mrs. Gurney's sister had her ambition realised too for it was also sung at her wedding.

Spiritual insight into the meaning of hymns isn't always easy. However, in his book, "The Gospel in Hymns," Albert Bailey points out that in this hymn, "the Lord Jesus Christ is given two titles that are of special significance in marriage - *perfect love* and *perfect life*." He concludes that these titles speak of two great ideals which are important in every marriage; motive and performance. If these ideals are honoured and obeyed they will yield joy and peace in marriage.

Perhaps it's also worth noting that Mrs. Gurney certainly brought out the truth that human love cannot begin to compare with God's love; which "transcends all human thought."

Mrs. Gurney died in 1932 and the London Times printed a tribute to her in the words with which I began this story. "Thousands of people at thousands of weddings must have sung, or heard sung, 'O Perfect Love,' without knowing that Mrs. Gurney wrote the hymn."

Rock Of Ages

The Rev. Augustus Montague Toplady, is one name which must be included in any list of the great hymn writers.

One day Toplady was travelling through the pleasant English countryside when a sudden, fierce storm sent him scurrying for shelter. He found it nearby, in the cleft of a great rock.

There are several places in the country where the locals will point positively to the exact location of Toplady's place of refuge; but since it is such a matter of dispute I'll refrain from favouring any one in particular.

The important thing is that the great man found the shelter he needed; and the wonderful thing for us is that, while there, and inspired by the situation and the surroundings, he penned those immortal lines: *"Rock of ages cleft for me, let me hide myself in thee."*

The Rev. Toplady was also the editor of a little religious periodical entitled, "The Gospel Magazine", and sometime later he used the lines he had written beneath the shelter of the rock in an article he had prepared for the paper.

In this he sought to establish the utter sinfulness of man; and the absolute necessity of receiving Christ's pardon. It was a totally scriptural essay, and to prove his point he compared the sins of the average individual to the national debt of England.

Toplady had calculated that a fifty year old man in his lifetime would be guilty of; one billion, five hundred and seventy-six million, eight hundred thousand sins. He quite rightly argued that it was humanly impossible for anyone to pay off such a staggering debt of iniquity, and therefore, sinners must needs avail themselves of the mercy and pardon of the Lord Jesus, who died upon the Cross to "redeem us from the curse of the law." He concluded the article with - "A living and dying prayer for the holiest believer in the world" - which contained the recently written hymn, *"Rock of ages."*

Just two years after these blessed words were first published, Augustus Toplady, at only 38 years of age, passed from this scene of time, into eternity; and to the everlasting shelter of *"The Rock of ages."*

Rock of Ages, cleft for me - Psalm 62:5-8.
Let me hide myself in Thee - Exodus 33:22.
Let the water and the blood - 1 John 5:6.
From Thy riven side which flowed - John 19:34.
Be of sin the double cure - 2 Kings 2:9-10.
Cleanse me from its guilt and power - Isaiah 1:18.

Not the labor of my hands - John 5:30 (first clause).
Can fulfil the law's demands - Matthew 5:17-18.
Could my zeal no respite know - Psalm 69:6 (first clause).
Could my tears forever flow - Psalm 6:6.
All for sin could not alone - Heb. 10:5-6.
Thou must save and Thou alone - Hebrews 10:8-10.

Nothing in my hand I bring - Isaiah 4:1.
Simply to Thy Cross I cling - Galatians 6:14.
Naked come to Thee for dress - Rom. 13:14 (first
   clause).
Helpless look to Thee for grace - Philippians 4:13.
Foul, I to the fountain fly - Psalm 2:7.
Wash me Saviour, or I die - John 13:8 (second
   clause).

While I draw this fleeting breath - Psalm 103:15-16.
When my eyelids close in death - Ecclesiastes 12:3-7.
When I soar to worlds unknown - John 14:2-3.
See Thee on Thy judgment throne - Matthew 25:31.
Rock of Ages cleft for me - 1 Corinthians 10-4 (third
   clause).
Let me hide myself in Thee - Psalm 16:1-8.

Stand Up, Stand Up For Jesus

To preach against slavery wasn't very popular in many parts of the U.S.A. during the early 1850's. An awful civil war, brought about by division over that very issue, was looming.

However, Dr. Dudley Tyng, the twenty-nine year old rector of the Church of the Epiphany in Philadelphia, believed slavery was "immoral and unchristian," so he denounced it.

He also believed that all men are sinners by nature and need to repent and be converted if they are ever to enter Heaven.

Dudley Tyng was no ordinary, fashionable church pastor and this bold, straight-forward denunication of sin disturbed his cultured and wealthy parishioners so much that by the end of his second year in the church many were demanding his removal.

Tyng resigned from the rich and fashionable assembly and formed his own "Church of the Covenant" which met for worship in a little meeting hall. He, with his wife and boys, went to live on the family farm outside Philadelphia.

At this time he also began giving lectures at the Philadelphia Y.M.C.A. Interest grew and thousands were converted to the Saviour. At one particular meeting held in Jayne's hall in March 1858, 5,000 men were present.

During his address Dr. Tyng said, "I must tell my master's errand and I would rather this right arm were amputated at the trunk than that I should come short of my duty in delivering God's message."

These words were strangely prophetic, for just the next week, while watching a horse-powered corn-sheller at work on the farm, he was caught in the wheels of the machinery and had his right arm badly mangled. A few days later it was necessary to amputate at the shoulder.

Tyng was dying and he realised it. As the loved ones gathered around his bed he took his father by the hand and addressed the old man, who was also a faithful preacher, in these words. *"Stand up for Jesus father, stand up for Jesus and tell my brethren of the ministry, wherever you meet them, to stand up for Jesus."* And thus he died.

The dying exhortation impressed another of Tyng's ministerial colleagues, the Rev. George Duffield. He took up the theme in a sermon preached the following Sunday from Eph. 6:14: "Stand therefore, having your loins girt about with truth." At the close of the sermon he read the words of this hymn he had composed just after Dr. Tyng's funeral.

"Stand up, stand up for Jesus
Ye soldiers of the cross
Lift high his royal banner
If must not suffer loss
From victory unto victory
His army He shall lead
'Til every foe is vanquished
And Christ is Lord indeed."

Sweet Hour Of Prayer

In Lord Tennyson's poem, "Morte D'Arthur" there's a line which reads, "More things are wrought by prayer than this world dreams of."

Certainly, nothing is accomplished in the Lord's work without prayer. It is the very life of it.

How much we need to pray, and yet, must we not confess - how little we do pray? I suppose then, every encouragement to prayer is valuable, even essential. This hymn is just that.

William Walford of Coleshill, England was a wood-carver by trade and the owner of a small trinket shop. He was also a devout Christian and often the guest preacher in the churches around the area where he lived.

One day, in 1842, the Reverend Thomas Salmon, a congregational minister, made his customary call at the shop of his friend. On this occasion, instead of showing the minister his beautiful collection of hand carved ornaments, Walford asked Mr. Salmon to write down the words of a poem he had just completed. The first verse went like this:-

"Sweet hour of prayer, sweet hour of prayer
That calls me from a world of care
And bids me at my Father's throne
Make all my wants and wishes known.

> *In seasons of distress and grief*
> *My soul has often found relief*
> *And oft' escaped the tempter's snare*
> *By thy return, sweet hour of prayer."*

Three years later the Reverend Salmon was in New York city and, while there, took the old wood-carver's poem along to the editor of the "New York Observer." As a result, *"Sweet hour of prayer"* appeared in the issue for September 1845.

Nothing happened for another fourteen years. Then the famous composer, William Bradbury, set the poem to music and turned it into one of the most famous hymns of all time.

Lifted on the wings of Bradbury's beautiful melody the words soon sped around the globe and in a short time were being sung by millions.

I mentioned earlier that William Walford had asked the minister to write down the words of his poem for him. The simple reason for this was that Walford himself was blind - he couldn't see how to write.

But he wasn't blind spiritually. The eyes of his soul could see clearly and perfectly. It took a rare insight to write such a meaningful and blessed sacred song as this.

Tell Me The Old Old Story

When William Gladstone was lecturing once on the subject of "Science, Industry, and Art," he said, "I do not mention any of these things as the great remedy for relieving the sorrow of human life and combating the evils which defile the world. If I am asked what is the remedy for these things, I must point to something which, in a well-known hymn, is called the 'old, old story', told of in an old, old book, and taught with an old, old teaching, which is the greatest gift ever given to mankind." A tremendous tribute, from a great statesman, to the lady who penned the words of this hymn.

Katherine Arabella Hankey was the daughter of a prosperous banker. She belonged to a group who sought to apply the ethics of Christ to personal, social, political and national affairs, and, like her father, showed great interest in people who were less fortunate than herself. She devoted much time to Bible teaching, especially among the factory girls of that day, and her efforts were rewarded in that many of her students became leaders in Christian work.

In 1866 Katherine, or Kate as she was better known, suffered a serious illness which required a lengthy convalescence. As she lay thinking of those who had been blessed by her telling of the story of redemption, she longed for someone to come in and tell her the old, old story. As a result she wrote a two-part, 50-verse poem on the life and work of our Lord. Part 1 was called, "The Story Wanted" and contained the words of this hymn *'Tell me the old, old story.'* Part 2, entitled "The Story Told" included a companion song 'I love to tell the story.'

Though written especially for children, *"The old, old story"* has been translated into more languages than almost any other children's hymn. The blessing of it has gone far beyond those for whom it was intended, for people of all ages and in all circumstances have known its touch. It seems clear then, that Katherine Hankey's intention was more than fulfilled. Speaking of the purpose behind the hymn she said "God's remedy for sin is something I want to understand, and I want to hear it often, lest I forget it. As weak as I am, I cannot think too well or too fast. I need to have the story explained to me as a little child."

"Tell me the old, old story" has a beautiful, gently flowing, and easily remembered tune. It was composed by Dr. William Howard Doane, whose interests included cotton manufacturing, woodworking, and the invention of a lot of the machinery used in those businesses.

Of the melody he composed to accompany these words he said, "I was attending the International Convention of the Young Men's Christian Association. Among those present was Major-General Russell, then in command of the English forces during the Irish home rule excitement. When the General rose to speak, he did not discuss the Irish situation, as we had expected. Simply and very softly he said, 'I merely want to read a very beautiful poem which should be the dominant theme undergirding everything we do here.' Then he read the words of Miss Hankey's hymn. At the end of the poem, General Russell was too emotional to speak."

"So impressed was I with the words that I requested a copy. Later, when travelling between the Glen Falls House and Crawford House in the White Mountains, I composed a tune for the words and added a simple little chorus. That evening, in the hotel parlours, we sang *'Tell me the old, old story,'* to my new tune."

Tell me the old, old story
Of unseen things above,
Of Jesus and His glory,
Of Jesus and His love.
Tell me the story simply,
As to a little child;
For I am weak and weary,
And helpless and defiled.

Tell me the old, old story,
Tell me the old, old story,
Tell me the old, old story
Of Jesus and His love.

There Is A Fountain Filled With Blood

Mention has already been made, in this book, of William Cowper, English poet and hymn writer who lived from 1731 until 1800.

It was Cowper, working in collaboration with the great John Newtown, who compiled and produced "Olney Hymns", a publication to which he personally contributed at least sixty-four original hymns. His most famous is *"There is a fountain filled with blood,"* and before we can tell the story it's necessary to set the scene by looking briefly at the life of the man who composed it.

William Cowper was born at Great Berkhampstead in Hertfordshire in November 1731. His mother died when he was only six years old and this tragedy left a life-long scar of grief. When he was ten he was sent to boarding school and there his suffering was added to by the cruelty of the older boys. However, he survived and at eighteen began to study law. Although he passed all the bar examinations he never achieved much success in his profession. In nine years of law practice, so-called, Cowper never once felt worthy to serve people nor could he manage to attract business for himself.

A clerkship in the House of Lords was arranged for him, but still he felt unfit for the task and was in such misery that he made several attempts to take his own life. The failure of these suicide attempts, compounded by two unhappy love affairs, increased his feelings of self contempt so that as he walked the streets he felt that all eyes were fixed upon him in scorn.

Because of the suicidal tendencies William Cowper was confined for a brief period in St. Albans Asylum and, remarkably, it was during this time in the mental hospital that his famous hymn was written.

A visiting relative sought to ease the sick man's depression by telling him of Jesus' power to save. Cowper burst into tears saying, "It is the first time that I have seen a ray of hope." When the friend had gone the poet opened his Bible at random and read from Romans ch. 3, v. 25: "Whom God hath set forth to be a propitiation through faith in his blood."

This Scriptural account of the redemptive work of Christ touched Cowper's heart, enabling him to testify, "There shone upon me the full beams of the sufficiency of the atonement that Christ has made, my pardon in His blood, the fulness and completeness of my justification; and in a moment I believed and received the gospel."

So thrilled was he by his new-found hope that he described it in verse, basing it on the words of Zechariah ch. 13, v. 1: "In that day there shall be a fountain opened up for sin and uncleanness."

It was William Cowper's hope that other troubled souls would be helped by his hymn.

Surely it must be said that he has succeeded far beyond his wildest expectations. How many countless thousands have been helped, blessed and encouraged by the singing of "There is a fountain filled with blood." Personally, I never like to conduct a gospel meeting without singing at least one hymn about the blood of Christ, and this is one of my favourites.

The great "prince of preachers" Charles Haddon Spurgeon was so taken with the words that instructions were given for some of the lines to be inscribed on his tomb. To this day visitors to the Spurgeon grave at Norwood cemetery, South London, can read:

> *"E'er since by faith I saw the stream*
> *Thy flowing wounds supply,*
> *Redeeming love has been my theme,*
> *And shall be till I die."*

What better way to sum up the whole theme of the hymn than by quoting:

> *"Dear dying Lamb! Thy precious blood*
> *Shall never lose its power,*
> *Till all the ransomed church of God*
> *Be saved to sin no more."*

There Is A Green Hill Far Away

The Cathedral Church of St. Columb, in Londonderry, N. Ireland, occupies the highest ground within the old walled city. The tall spire atop the building makes a fine outline against the blue sky on a clear day; nothing else interrupts the view.

St. Columb's has stood on its commanding site for 350 years and is fair steeped in history.

Within its Chapter House are a host of relics dating back to the time of the famous seige. Then it was that upwards of 30,000 Protestants from the surrounding area packed into the ancient city; to seek shelter behind its stout walls from the approaching armies of King James II.

The walls of the Chapter House are lined with cupboards and cabinets, each crammed with memorabilia of the siege. The locks and keys of the sturdy wooden gates; pistols and muskets used in defence of liberty; even a piece from the tree, down which a traitor is said to have escaped; are all there to delight and amaze.

But all these took little of my attention when I visited the place just recently. My interest was taken by a picture which has pride of place on one wall. It's the picture of a woman; modest of dress, saintly of face, and, by all reports, gracious of spirit.

Cecil Frances Alexander is remembered with affection in the city which was once her home.

A beautiful, stained-glass, memorial window in the baptistry of the cathedral pays eloquent tribute to her life and witness.

Mrs. Alexander lived and worked for the sake of children, and so it is fitting that the window should be placed there. The scene portrayed in gorgeous colours depicts the Saviour's love and care for little ones; and the simple inscription at the bottom reads:

"In grateful memory of Cecil Frances Alexander, wife of William, Bishop Alexander. She died in this city on 12th October 1895."

Beside the window a large plaque with the appearance of a tapestry displays one of Mrs. Alexander's finest pieces of poetry "A Prayer for this Cathedral church." It includes this telling verse:

> *Be here O Christ of our Salvation*
> *As once in Israels temple fair*
> *Cleanse Thou from sin our poor oblation*
> *And make this house, a house of prayer.*

It is for her poetry that Mrs. Alexander will be best remembered, especially the song written for children.

As early as 1848 she published her famous little volume: "Hymns for little children," and she dedicated thus:

"To my little Godsons, I inscribe these lines hoping that the language of the verse, which children love, may help to impress on their minds what they are, what I have promised for them, and what they must seek to be."

There are many, like myself, who would not be in favour of the taking of vows by God-parents; but it seems clear that at least Mrs. Alexander took them seriously.

She went to great pains to write some 41 hymns for the spiritual edification of her little friends and it's interesting to note the plan she adopted.

As the basis of her songbook she took the catechism; and wrote verses on each section of it, thus hoping to impress its truths upon young hearts. There are hymns on the Trinity, Baptism, The Creed, the Ten Commandments, and The Lord's Prayer.

Among the well known favourites are *"Do no sinful action"*; *"All things bright and beautiful"*; *"Once in royal David's City"* and *"There is a green hill far away."*

The inspiration for this last hymn is said to have come from the neighbourhood where she lived.

The Alexanders lived in the Bishop's Palace, almost beside the cathedral. The house had a commanding view out over the city walls to the green hills beyond. No wonder then that she was inspired to write:

> *"There is a green hill, far away*
> *Without a city wall*
> *Where the dear Lord was crucified*
> *Who died to save us all."*

By 1872 "Hymns for little children" had sold 414,000 copies, clear evidence of its blessing to multitudes.

Mrs. Alexander died on October 12th 1895 some 16 years before her husband.

He eventually became Archbishop of Armagh and Primate of all Ireland; and when that appointment took place moved to live in the city of Armagh, ecclesiastical seat of Ireland.

But the Primate was a Derry man at heart and longed to come home again someday. It is said that he always wished to be buried in his home city with his feet towards the river Foyle. His wish was granted.

On that great day, when we all stand before the judgment throne of heaven, surely all will rise up and call her, "blessed."

The Alexanders lie buried on the slope of that "green hill" which inspired the writing of the lovely hymn. A plain white marble cross marks the spot.

Beneath the name Cecil Frances Alexander is written in brackets
"(C.F.A., Hymn writer)."

The Solid Rock

It's many years now since I first heard a preacher recite the rather unusual couplet:

"On Christ the solid rock I stand;
All other rocks are shamrocks!"

He was, of course, quoting a parody on the chorus of the hymn *"On Christ the solid rock I stand."* What a fine hymn it is. Bishop Bickersteth, himself an outstanding hymnist, called it "a grand hymn of faith." There's no doubt that his assessment is right.

"The Solid Rock," to give the hymn its proper title, was written in 1834 and first appeared, anonymously, in leaflets and newspapers. Very quickly, considerable debate arose as to the identity of the author, and so the man responsible, Mr. Edward Mote, decided to acknowledge his workmanship.

Explaining how the idea for the hymn came - on his way to work - Mote said, "I began to meditate on the gracious experience of the Christian. Soon the chorus, and then the words of the first verse came to mind."

The following Sunday, coming out of morning worship, he was invited to a friends home to encourage his wife who was critically ill. He went to the home in the early evening, and after spending some time comforting the dying woman, was asked to join in family worship. It was the custom in the house to sing a hymn, read the scripture, and pray. As the man of the house searched in vain for a hymn book, Edward Mote said, "I have some verses in my pocket. If you like we can sing them," and they did.

The words struck a responsive chord in the heart of the sick woman and, as a consequence, her husband requested a copy for her.

"Back at home," continues the author, "I sat by the fireside, musing on the sick lady's reaction to the words I had written; and soon the entire hymn was clear in my mind." This new, enlarged version was committed to paper and a copy made for the dying friend. Later, he thought that since the hymn had been such a blessing and comfort to this dying woman, maybe it would be of help to others as well. So, a thousand leaflets were printed for distribution.

Edward Mote was born in London on January 21st, 1797. His background appeared to be far from Christian. As a boy he had no interest in the things of God. In fact, so ignorant of spiritual matters was he that he didn't even know there was a God. His parents were of no help to him. They kept a public house and sent their son to a school where the Bible was neither taught nor permitted. On Sundays, instead of attending church, he and his friends of the neighbourhood spent their time playing in the streets.

However, for some reason which is not known, Edward began attending church when he became a cabinet makers' apprentice. About this time he went to hear the famous preacher, Rev. John Hyatt at Tottenham Court Road Chapel. He records that the sermon made him "think on his ways," and two years later he came into the experience of salvation.

Eventually, he felt called to preach the gospel which he now believed and was instrumental in the building of at least one church. It is evident that he exercised a faithful ministry there for when he died the congregation erected a plaque which read, "For 26 years the beloved pastor of this church, preaching Christ and Him crucified, as all the sinner can need, and all the saint can desire."

Assurance and security were Edward Mote's constant companions throughout his long life. Even when his health began to fail and he was approaching death he felt a renewed confidence in the merit of the blood of Christ. Just before he died, in 1874, he said, "I think I am nearing Port. But the truths I have preached I am living upon, and they will do to die upon. Ah! the precious blood! The precious blood which takes away all my sins; it is this which makes peace with God", and thus he said farewell to Earth . . .

"Dressed in His righteousness alone
Faultless to stand before the throne!"

The Sweet By And By

Just like all the rest of us, composer Joseph Webster had his off days. So when he walked into the office of his friend Dr. Sandford Bennett, the doctor instinctively knew that the musician was down in the dumps.

"What's the trouble now," Bennett asked Webster who appeared rather melancholy. "Oh, nothing," came the dejected reply. "Everything will be alright by and by."

Dr. Bennett turned back to his desk where he wrote prescriptions as a profession and verse as a hobby. "By and by", he mused. *The sweet by and by.* He paused, looked over at Webster who by this time was warming himself at the stove and then reached for his writing paper and pen.

The man at the stove, Joseph Philbrick Webster was an out and out musician. In the east, where he was born in 1819, he had been an active member of the Handel and Hayden society; and a prolific composer of popular songs. In his early thirties he made the great move west, first to Indiana and then in 1857 to Elkhorn, Wisconsin, where he eventually settled.

When the verse writing physician, Sanford Fillmore Bennett moved to the same town in 1861, it was natural that the two should strike up a partnership. After six years Bennett knew Webster like a song-book and he soon learned that the best remedy for his partner's bouts of gloom was a batch of verses to be set to music.

But on that particular day in 1867, the clever doctor had no such remedy in stock. However, Webster's casual remark had given him a theme and quickly he had gone to work.

While the physician wrote hastily at his desk two other townsfolk joined the musician at the stove. In a few minutes Bennett handed Webster three verses and a chorus; and in less time than it had taken the doctor to write the words the composer set it to music.

He gave the melody a few rounds on his violin and the four men sang the new hymn for the first time.

There's a land that is fairer than day,
*   And by faith we can see it afar;*
For the Father waits over the way,
*   To prepare us a dwelling-place there.*

In the sweet by and by,
*   We shall meet on that beautiful shore.*
In the sweet by and by,
*   We shall meet on that beautiful shore.*

What A Friend We Have In Jesus

Only the Lord and the man in question really know what burdens of sorrow and affliction were heaped upon the writer of this great hymn. One thing we do know however, is that this beautiful and blessed hymn would never have been penned if the author had not known such trouble.

The man was Joseph Scriven and he was born near Banbridge, in the heart of the rolling hills of County Down, here in Ulster.

After graduating from Dublin's famous "Trinity College" he seemed set for a brilliant career and a happy life for he was also engaged to be married.

But then tragedy struck! His fiancee was accidentally drowned on the very eve of their wedding and Joseph Scriven was plunged into his first great experience of sorrow. It was this tragedy which brought him to a personal knowledge of Jesus Christ.

In 1845 Scriven sailed for Canada to start life anew and, hopefully, to leave all his sorrows behind. But it was not to be for ill-health dogged him and he was forced to return to Ireland after only two months.

Two years later he again set sail for Canada to take up a teaching post and later graduated to the position of private tutor to the children of a military captain.

Life, at last, seemed worth living and prospects were continually improving. He met and fell in love with a charming young woman of twenty-three and soon they were engaged to be married.

However, bitter disappointment was once more to be his lot for the young lady was suddenly stricken with a serious illness and died.

Cheated, for the second time, out of the prospects of a happy marriage by the cruel hand of death, Scriven, quite naturally, became the victim of severe depression and declining health. But despite all this he never gave up his personal faith in the Saviour.

By this time he had settled in Port Hope, Ontario and managed a small dairy there. He became known as the local "Good Samaritan" helping the poor and under-privileged, sharing his food with the needy and often giving them clothing.

However, all these good deeds may well have been forgotten if Joseph Scriven had not written twenty-four lines of poetry to comfort his mother who was suffering a serious illness. Through trial and affliction Scriven had come to know the Lord in a very personal way, not only as Saviour but also as a friend.

From the heart he could write:

> *"What a friend we have in Jesus,*
> *All our sins and griefs to bear,*
> *What a privilege to carry*
> *Everything to God in prayer."*

As I say, Scriven wrote these words to comfort his ageing mother at a time of illness. He had not seen her since he said "goodbye" over ten years before and wasn't able to make the long journey back home to be with her. So he wrote *What a friend we have in Jesus* and sent it with the prayer that it would remind her of "the never failing friend," Christ Jesus. I'm sure it did.

Joseph Scriven never intended his poem to be published but a friend who visited him during his last illness discovered the lines and asked "Who wrote those beautiful words?" Scriven's modest reply was "The Lord and I did it between us."

Soon it was published in "The Port Hope Guide" a local newspaper. Remarkably a copy of that newspaper was used to wrap a parcel destined for an address in New York City. When the recipient unwrapped his parcel he caught sight of Scriven's poem and arranged to have it published. Eventually it was seen by German-American composer, Charles Converse and very soon his simple, plaintive melody gave wings of song to Joseph Scriven's telling words.

Thus an Irish-American and a German-American were used of God to bring blessing and encouragement to millions.

When I Survey The Wondrous Cross

When teenager Isaac Watts complained to his father about the monotonous way Christians in England sang the Old Testament Psalms, his father, a leading deacon, snapped back, "All right young man you give us something better."

To Isaac Watts the singing of God's praise was the form of worship nearest to Heaven and he went on to argue "It's performance among us is the worst on earth." Young Isaac accepted his father's challenge and eventually wrote a total of more than 600 hymns, earning him the title "The father of English hymnody."

Even as a child Isaac had shown a passion for poetry, rhyming such mundane things as everyday conversation. His serious-minded father, after several warnings, decided to spank the rhyming nonsense out of his son. But the tearful Isaac helplessly replied, "Oh father do some pity take and I will no more verses make."

However, choirs, congregations and individual Christians rejoice to this day that the young lad did not keep his impromptu promise. If he had, none of us would have the thrill of singing such all-time favourites as "Oh God our help in ages past", "Am I a soldier of the cross" or "Joy to the world".

In his hymns, Isaac Watts takes the Word of God, of which he must have been a diligent student, and distills it for us so that all its wisdom, beauty and comfort are set before us with plainness and power. No wonder, then, that C.H. Spurgeon's grandfather, himself a great preacher and in the line of the puritans, would sing nothing else but the hymns of the great Isaac Watts.

The hymn we have chosen to consider is *"When I survey the wondrous cross."* It has been called, "The very best hymn in the English language" and in it Watts, using only 16 lines, paints a soul-stirring picture of the Saviour's death on the cross coupled with the whole-hearted response of the believer to such amazing love.

Here in Ulster it's a favourite with many congregations, especially on those occasions when they meet around the Lord's table to remember His death.

How blessed to reflect on the finished work of Christ Jesus, as summed up in those lines:-

> *"See, from His head, His hands, His feet,*
> *Sorrow and love flow mingled down;*
> *Did e'er such love and sorrow meet,*
> *Or thorns compose so rich a crown?"*

And how enriching to be able to voice our reconsecration to the Lord's service in the words:

> *"Were the whole realm of nature mine,*
> *That were an offering far too small;*
> *Love so amazing, so divine,*
> *Demands my soul, my life, my all."*

The Old Rugged Cross

I can remember distinctly the first time I heard this great hymn.

As a young lad I went with my mother on what we called "a bus run." That's a special outing, usually to the seaside, and travelling - in those days before cars were so plentiful - by special, privately-hired bus. A great treat indeed!

To occupy the time on these jolly jaunts there would always be a bit of a sing-song. The popular tunes of the day, the beautiful old Irish ballads and everyones' favourites would be enthusiastically aired.

To this day I carry a clear mental picture of an old cream and green bus, chugging its smokey way along a twisting country road, its cargo of carefree passengers packed like sardines and singing like thrushes.

But even more clear is the memory of the hymn, for, always on those occasions the singing would end and the day be brought to a close - as if to pour a sanctifying oil over the whole proceedings - with a hushed and reverent rendering of a favourite hymn. The one which I can remember above all others is *"The old rugged cross."*

The author and composer, Rev. George Bennard, testifies that this hymn was not born in haste. He prayerfully read everything the Bible has to say about the cross of Christ and thus became convinced that the cross was not just a religious symbol. It was, rather, the very heart of the gospel of the Lord Jesus - the only gospel by which poor siners are saved.

George Bennard believed that redemption for man only comes through Christ's sacrifice on the accursed tree.

Gripped by this vision of redemption, the theme of "The old rugged cross" came to him. The words however, were not written until after a two-week waiting period which he described as "a test of faith."

He had already composed that unique melody, and now the words were wedded to it - a beautiful and perfect union.

Nathaniel Olson sums it up nicely in his book "Hymns of faith" when he describes it as "words of truth on wings of melody."

References

"Hymns of Faith" by Nathanael Olsen. Ideals Pub. Company. Co. Milwaukee, Wis. (1975).

"A hymn is born" by Clint Bonner. Broadman Press. Nashville, Tenn. (1959).

"Faith for the family." Bob Jones Univ. Press. Greenville, S.C.

"Out of the depths." (Autobiography of John Newton), Moody Press. Chicago.

"Encyclopaedia Britannica" (1969).

"Hymns for little children" by Mrs. C. F. Alexander. (Courtesy of the Dean of Derry).

"Crusader Hymn Stories." Hope Publication Co.; Chicago (1967).

"No surrender" by Tony Gray. MacDonald and James (1975).

"Our daily bread." Radio Bible Class. Grand Rapids, Michigan.

"Time Magazine."